Mother Teresa

Barbara Kramer

 NATIONAL
GEOGRAPHIC

Washington, D.C.

Reader

For my editors, Shelby and Laura —B.K.

Designed by Yay! Design

Trade paperback ISBN: 978-1-4263-3347-7
Reinforced library binding ISBN: 978-1-4263-3348-4

The author and publisher gratefully acknowledge the expert content review of this book by Kathryn Spink, author of *Mother Teresa: An Authorized Biography,* and the literacy review of this book by Mariam Jean Dreher, professor of reading education, University of Maryland, College Park.

Photo Credits
CO: Corbis; GI: Getty Images
Cover: Tim Graham/GI, (background), Arsgera/Shutterstock; 1, Mere Teresa/Bridgeman Images; 3, Keystone Features/GI; 4, Bettmann/GI; 5, Tim Graham/GI; 6 (UP), Vittoriano Rastelli/CO via GI; 6 (LO), Tim Graham/GI; 8, Hans Hildenbrand/National Geographic Creative; 9, Vittoriano Rastelli/CO via GI; 10-11, Vittoriano Rastelli/CO via GI; 12 (UP), Floortje/GI; 12 (LO), Kenneth Sponsler/Shutterstock; 13 (UP), JTB Photo/UIG via GI; 13 (CTR), biancardi/Shutterstock; 13 (LO), Vittoriano Rastelli/CO via GI; 14, Vittoriano Rastelli/CO via GI; 16, Vittoriano Rastelli/CO via GI; 17, Zvonimir Atletic/Shutterstock; 18, Vittoriano Rastelli/CO via GI; 19 (UP), Vittoriano Rastelli/CO via GI; 19 (LO), Earl & Nazima Kowall/GI; 20, JTB Photo/UIG via GI; 21, Keystone/GI; 22, Saikat Paul/Pacific Press/LightRocket via GI; 23 (UP), Terry Fincher.Photo Int/Alamy Stock Photo; 23 (LO), Friedrich Stark/Alamy Stock Photo; 24 (UP), pirtuss/Shutterstock; 24 (CTR), Dinodia Photo/GI; 24 (LO), paresh3d/GI; 25 (UP LE), traveler1116/GI; 25 (UP RT), catwalker/Shutterstock; 25 (CTR), AFP/GI; 25 (LO), Jean-Claude FRANCOLON/Gamma-Rapho via GI; 26, Dave Norris/Toronto Star via GI; 27, Jean-Claude FRANCOLON/Gamma-Rapho via GI; 28-29, nafterphoto/Shutterstock; 28, Mark Wilson/GI; 29, Allison Joyce/GI; 30, Franco Origlia/GI; 31 (UP LE), Dinodia Photo/GI; 31 (UP RT), pirtuss/Shutterstock; 31 (LO LE), Zvonimir Atletic/Shutterstock; 31 (LO RT), spatuletail/Shutterstock; 32 (UP LE), Allison Joyce/GI; 32 (UP RT), Zvonimir Atletic/Shutterstock; 32 (LO LE), Tim Graham/GI; 32 (LO RT), Saikat Paul/Pacific Press/LightRocket via GI; vocabulary box art, spatuletail/Shutterstock

**National Geographic supports K–12 educators with ELA Common Core Resources.
Visit natgeoed.org/commoncore for more information.**

Printed in the United States of America
18/WOR/1

Table of Contents

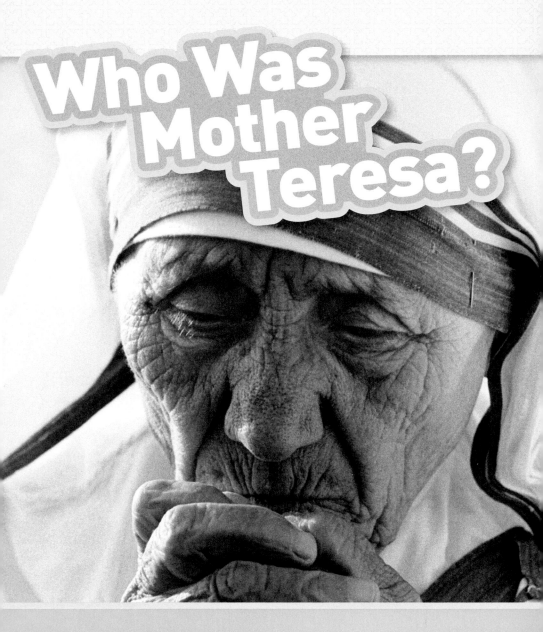

Who Was Mother Teresa?

Mother Teresa spent most of her life helping others. She fed the hungry. She nursed the sick and the dying.

She never wanted attention.
But people heard about her work.
They told other people. Mother
Teresa became famous around
the world.

Early Years

As a child, Mother Teresa was known as Agnes Gonxha Bojaxhiu (AG-nes gon-KHA boe-ya-JEE-oh).

Agnes on the day of her confirmation

In Her Own Words

"We can do no big things, only small things with great love."

She was born on August 26,
1910, in what is now Macedonia
(MASS–uh–DOE–knee–yah).
She grew up in the city of Skopje
(SKO–pee–ah).

a vegetable vendor in one of the streets of Skopje, where Agnes grew up

Agnes prayed with her family. She sang in the church choir. She liked to read and thought about becoming a writer.

Her parents taught her about kindness. Agnes and her mother took food to neighbors who had none. They helped others who were sick.

Agnes and her mother

Agnes's father was a successful businessman.

Agnes (right) had an older sister and an older brother.

Agnes's father died when she was about 8 years old. This left the family with little money. But Agnes and her mother kept helping others who had even less.

At church, 12-year-old Agnes heard about nuns who helped the poor. That was what she wanted to do.

Words to Know

NUNS: Women who live together and give their lives to working for their god

Mother Teresa

Agnes with her classmates

In Her Time

When Mother Teresa was a girl in Skopje in the 1910s, many things were different from how they are now.

TOYS AND GAMES: Children played games such as hide-and-seek. Girls jumped rope and played with rag dolls. Boys played marbles and enjoyed ball games.

TRANSPORTATION: People traveled on foot, on bicycles, or in horse-drawn carriages. For long distances, they went by boat or by train.

Skopje today

CULTURE: People walked along cobblestone streets to buy handmade goods from a small group of stores called a bazaar.

COMMUNICATION: People could mail letters from one of two post offices in the city. They could also have messages sent by telegraph, which was used before telephones came to the area.

CLOTHES: Young boys wore shorts and older boys wore long pants. Girls dressed in the latest styles, but for special occasions they wore traditional costumes of their country.

Agnes (left) and her sister are dressed in traditional costumes.

13

A New Life

This photo of Mother Teresa was taken a few days before she left for Ireland.

For six years, Agnes prayed about becoming a nun. When she was 18, she took the first step. She joined the Loreto (loh-RAY-toe) Sisters.

She began her training in Ireland. After six weeks, she was sent to India to work as a missionary (MISH-uh-ner-ee).

Words to Know

MISSIONARY: A person from a religious group who travels to another country to help people and teach about religion

NORTH AMERICA

Ireland

EUROPE

Macedonia

ASIA

ATLANTIC OCEAN

India

AFRICA

SOUTH AMERICA

INDIAN OCEAN

The trip from Ireland to India took five weeks by ship.

It takes many years to become a nun. Agnes got more training in India. She chose the name Teresa for her new life as a nun.

Sister Teresa (left) and another woman during their training to become nuns in Darjiling, India

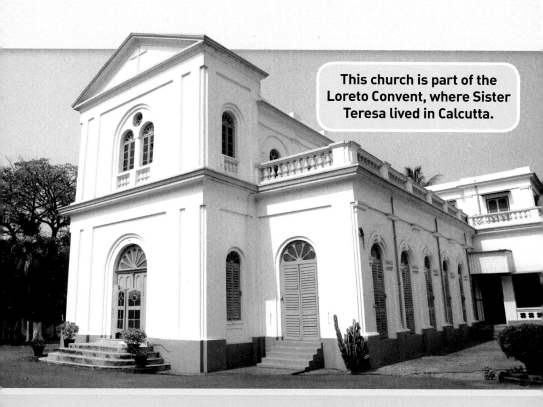

This church is part of the Loreto Convent, where Sister Teresa lived in Calcutta.

In 1931, Sister Teresa began teaching in the city then known as Calcutta. The school was inside the grounds of the convent where she lived. Her students said she made learning fun.

Words to Know

CONVENT: A place where nuns live, work, and pray together

In 1937, she made a vow, or promise, to be a nun for life. She became Mother Teresa.

Standing on the right is Mother Teresa, dressed in a nun's habit on the day she made a promise to be a nun for life.

In Her Own Words

"I am only a little pencil in God's hands."

She was happy. But outside the convent walls were people who had no food or homes. Mother Teresa believed her god was calling her to help those people.

Hungry children search for food in a pile of garbage.

19

Helping the Poor

In 1948, Mother Teresa left the convent. It was hard to leave her home and her friends. But she was ready to begin her work among the poor. In place of a nun's black habit, she wore a sari (SAR-ee). This was how many women of India dressed.

women wearing saris

A sari is made from one piece of fabric wrapped around the body. Mother Teresa's sari was white with three blue stripes.

Mother Teresa first opened a small school. Soon, other women came to work with her. They wanted to be nuns, too. In 1950, Mother Teresa and the nuns who helped her became known as Missionaries of Charity. They were now a new order, or group, of nuns.

nuns of the Missionaries of Charity

Words to Know

CHARITY: The act of giving to others in need

Mother Teresa in Calcutta, India, in 1979

The Missionaries of Charity Mother House in Calcutta was built in 1953. Mother Teresa lived there and is buried there.

6 COOL FACTS About Mother Teresa

1 As a child, Mother Teresa played an instrument called a mandolin (man-duh-LIN).

2 When Mother Teresa started her first school, she had no supplies and no school building. She held classes under a tree and used a stick to scratch the alphabet in the dirt.

3 In 1948, Mother Teresa became a citizen of India. It was the country she would call home.

Many countries around the world have put Mother Teresa on their postage stamps.

4

In 1979, Mother Teresa was awarded the Nobel (no-bell) Peace Prize. It is one of the world's most famous awards. It is given to someone who works for peace.

5

6

Mother Teresa worked hard, but she had fun, too. She smiled as she went about her work and she loved a good joke.

Spreading Love

Large crowds came to hear Mother Teresa speak about helping others.

In Her Own Words

"If there are poor on the moon, we shall go there, too."

Mother Teresa's work grew. In 1965, she began helping the poor in other countries.

As Mother Teresa got older, she had more and more health problems. But she never stopped working. She died on September 5, 1997. She was 87 years old.

Mother Teresa had a smile for everyone.

On September 4, 2016, Mother Teresa was named a saint. It meant she had lived a holy, or special, life.

1910

**Is born on
August 26**

1928

**Begins training
to become a nun**

1948

**Leaves the convent
and begins her work
among the poor**

The Missionaries of Charity carry on with Mother Teresa's work.

Today, there are more than 5,000 nuns in the Missionaries of Charity order. They want to keep doing the work Mother Teresa started.

1950
Starts her order, the Missionaries of Charity

1997
Dies on September 5

2016
Is named a saint on September 4

What in the World?

These pictures show items in Mother Teresa's life. Use the hints to figure out what's in the pictures. Answers on page 31.

1

HINT: Mother Teresa wore this dress made from one long piece of fabric.

2

INDIAN OCEAN

HINT: Mother Teresa became a citizen of this country.

Word Bank

India	convent	mandolin	tree	sari	stamps

3

HINT: Mother Teresa held classes under this in her first school.

4

HINT: Mother Teresa played music on this.

5

HINT: Nuns live, work, and pray in this place.

6

HINT: Mother Teresa's picture appears on these around the world.

Answers: 1. sari, 2. India, 3. tree, 4. mandolin, 5. convent, 6. stamps

CHARITY: The act of giving to others in need

CONVENT: A place where nuns live, work, and pray together

MISSIONARY: A person from a religious group who travels to another country to help people and teach about religion

NUNS: Women who live together and give their lives to working for their god